# INTRODUCTIOI

A career in Nursing has blessed me with the opportunity to witness the very length, width and depth of the human experience. I have participated in life and death from literally before the first breath to after the last gasp. I have experienced first-hand the very worst and the very best of the human condition; lives won, lives lost, lives given away and lives changed in a moment and a twinkling of an eye. I have seen life and death cheated, feared, welcomed and treated as trivial as a signature on a piece of paper. I have seen Love that knows no bounds and unfathomable hate. Most of all, I have seen life in all its glory as a nurse and would not change one second of it. With this thought comes a wandering as to what has kept me in the game. I am sure it was not the money, prestige, or gratitude. It was my patients and coworkers. Moreover, I think it was the people and the times when I was able to laugh at myself, and those around me. It is that very part of nursing, the very best part, I hope to share with you. The part of my nursing career that made it a little easier to get up each day and do what we do. I hope it will in some way enrich you as it is has me and maybe help you chuckle a little when times get hard.

This book is for all the medical personnel, i.e., nurses, physicians, residents, respiratory therapists, and nursing students. Humor and the ability to laugh at oneself is essential for a health care professional to maintain some reasonable form of sanity. Working in such a high stress environment mandates some form of stress relief. For a health care professional it most often manifests in a way a nonprofessional would consider at best odd, at worst morbid, and maybe disrespectful. I can assure you that this book is not meant to degrade those who have lost their lives, a loved one, or who have had to live with severe and debilitating injuries from unexpected events in their lives. In many cases, the ways health professional's keep their sanity in such emotion filled work environments turns out to be harmless and even a little humorous.

I have recorded, from time to time, some funny and odd experiences from my nursing career. I would like to share them with you in the following pages. I hope that you will be able to chuckle at the similarities if you are a health worker, or at least be amused at the things nurses see and experience in their careers if you are not. Please accept my apologies. My writing skills are lacking to say the least. Again, it is my hope that whoever reads this will understand that patients are why we all do this. Patients always come first, and should always be cared for in the most diligent and dignified way possible. I hope you enjoy this collection of humorous and true short stories.

**THANK YOU,** I would like to take this opportunity to thank my husband and my parents. Without their support, I would never have been able to return to nursing school with a one year old and a three year old at home. They have been very supportive over the years and encouraging. Without their support, I would not have been brave enough to go back to school.

Special thanks to my husband, who has listened repeatedly over the years to my complaints about work, dried my tears, and soothed my frustrations without a whimper. He did this with love while always giving his support.

Thanks to Dr. John Ortolani, trauma resident, who first gave me the idea to do this. Our swapping of humorous tales was a wonderful inspiration. Without his encouragement, I would not have been brave enough to make this attempt at writing, as feeble as it is. Thanks also to Dr. Baker, MD for his guidance and invaluable advice on writing and self-publishing.

Thank you all, from the bottom of my heart for all of your support and encouraging words over the years. Mom, Dad, Steve, Jordan, Jared, Dr. Ortolani, Dr. Baker, Dr. Farris, Dr. Rudderow, Dr. Diaz, Dr. Drake, and Dr. Pressley thank you from the bottom of my heart and I love you all dearly. I would not be who I am without my wonderful, crazy, and intense Neuro/Trauma ICU family. We really are a family and I love you all.

So, here it is...

# CHAPTER 1

## WHY??

Although I cannot support it with data I suspect that some people go into nursing mainly for the money. Granted it is not the greatest pay but there are not many occupations where a two-year degree and registry can earn you a starting salary well above the national average and practically guarantee a position immediately or even before graduation. Some chose nursing as a way to help people while making a decent living. Nursing instructors either accidently or by design forget what it is really like and all too often paint nursing in the best light possible. All I can say about that is, it doesn't take very long to wake up from that fairy-tale land and realize you're in the real world.

As a new nurse, I had this angelic view of nursing. I put doctors on a pedestal and thought everyone would thank me, appreciate everything kind thing I did and admire me. Wow! Was I looking through rose-colored glasses. Well, I woke up and discovered long hours, weekends, 12 and 16-hour shifts with little help and less appreciation. There are the missed holidays, kid's birthdays, school- events, not to mention the cleaning of every excrement that can possibly be secreted or projected from the human body

More than a few patients think they have checked into a Holiday Inn and you are there to be a maid to them and their family. Nurses are cursed, attacked by patients, and visitors and often disrespected. So why do it? Why keep coming back? The reasons are many and varied, basically, we love our patients. Nurses want to be their voice when they are unable. We love the thrill and a challenge. Nurses want a chance of actually making a positive difference in someone's life. Although we can be adrenaline junkies, we believe that a life is worth the effort no matter what the cost. So to keep doing this job, it is pertinent to develop a sense of humor and find ways of relieving stress. Stress relief for a nurse is very different than the average person and often results in very humorous and odd situations.

It is  these times that I would like to share with you in the hopes you may get a chuckle or two and in the end maybe get to know us nurses a little better. Who knows it may be a little bit of a stress relief for you.

# CHAPTER 2

## The Beginning

I often thought about going to school to be a nurse. However, I worried I might not be able to pass the classes, especially Anatomy. I'll admit it now, if I had studied nursing fresh out of high school, I would not have put in the required amount of time one needs nor would I have appreciated the opportunity. So I went on to college, obtained another degree, married, and had two wonderful sons.

My husband, in the fall of 1994 decided to take some courses to keep up-to-date with his job. By chance while with my husband at the college, I saw a sign on a bulletin board for nursing classes and on a whim, I registered for the RN program.

*First semester, oh no, the dreaded anatomy class.* Both sons admitted to the hospital with respiratory issues on my first day of class. They were one and four at the time. I had a strict but wonderful instructor who taught us so much. I graduated with an A.A.S. Degree in Nursing( RN) in 1996, Magnum Cum Laude, and thought I would change the world.

# CHAPTER 3

## REALITY

My first nursing position was in a 32-bed step down unit, at a small rural hospital. The unit had seven beds with cardiac telemetry and was equipped to take four ventilated patients. I was on orientation and by 0715 I realized, I was not in Kansas anymore. My first indication that the real world and that of nursing school were not the same, dawned on me when I received my first instructions. An experienced LPN who was orienting me, who I still thank God for every day, informed me I needed to go clean up my patient. For those who do not know, that means they have had a BM (bowel movement). My first response was, "OK, I'll get the aide they can clean him up. After she finished laughing, she said in as kind way as possible, "Honey, you are the aide." Still like an idiot, I said, "but in nursing school, I was told an aide would be available to do *those*" jobs. Again more laughing, laughing. Lesson learned, there is nothing like on the job training.

# CHAPTER 4

## Enlightenment

They also do not teach you how not to laugh when you get report on a patient and the nurse tells you there is a vibrator up the rectum and it disappeared into the rectum and X-Rays later confirm. The patient is wheeled off the elevator and as he rolls by we hear a muffled, hmmmmm. The doctor quietly says, "Please call me when the battery dies." The patient pleaded, "Please don't tell my wife about this." I politely and quickly say, "I won't", close the door and walk very briskly down the hall so we can all die laughing. Some batteries last a very long time. Every hour or so I would stick my head in the room and listen for the characteristic "hmmmmmmmm". It was still humming when I left that morning, poor guy.

# CHAPTER 5

## Is It Legible?

We had a doctor who for over 50 years arrived precisely at 4:00 am every morning except for 5:00 am on Sunday's, and would arrive to make rounds. He swam at the local YMCA first then came to the hospital. He was at least 70 years old. If he didn't write the same orders each morning, we would not have been able to read a word he wrote. I would make him stay put until I checked all the charts in case he did write an order and I could not read them.

One morning he got away from me and I had to call him, after explaining to him that I could not read an order he had just written. He was quiet for a minute and then said *"me either,"* just order what I usually do. Please remember nurses are the voice for our patients and their advocate. We are the ones at the bedside 24- hours a day. We see things physicians do not. We are their eyes. I have worked with wonderful physicians over the years. Never be afraid to call or question a doctor or their orders if it is in the best interest of the patient. It is better to be yelled at for calling, than not calling at all.

# CHAPTER 6

## The Black Cloud Beginning

I always have a plan when I work as charge nurse, just so everyone knows where to go and what to do in case all hell breaks loose. At this time in my career, I have less than one year of experience and I am the most experienced nurse on the floor so by default I am the charge nurse. It does not seem to matter to management that I have never coded a patient, or even seen an actual code, except on the television series ER. I watched ER faithfully through nursing school and was very disappointed when I started to work and realized none of the real life doctors looked anything like George Clooney!

On this particular night everything is going along fine, I'm checking on all my patient's, all 32, because we are full, we seem to always be full when I work of course. There are four nurses plus the charge who doesn't take patients, but who is responsible for putting all the charts together, watching the monitor's, calling physicians, taking care of complaints,(actually what they can Clinical Team Leaders Now), etc.

As a rule I, try to stick my head in the rooms every hour or so, especially those who are not on a monitor just to stay on top of things. I had just made rounds, talked to the lady in Room 475 who had refused her NG Tube (nasogastric tube) and walked back to the nurse's station, when an aide shouted," **ROOM 475 ISN'T BREATHING YOU NEED TO COME CHECK ON HER"!!!!**

In all of my extensive seven months of experience, I deduced the aide must be mistaken, I was just in the room and spoke with her. So I walk promptly into the room, said her name, no response, checked for a pulse and promptly said," see, she has a pulse and gently shook her". There was no response. I checked for a pulse again, I feel a pulse. I check my pulse then her pulse and realize, it is my pulse I am feeling. She did not have a pulse, she was *NOT* breathing. We called a Code-Blue, and started chest compressions.

When the code team arrived, we stepped back so they could take over. I had to climb into the windowsill as to not be in the way of team. The doctor wanted to know the circumstance so I very professionally started crying and saying, *I don't know, I just don't know, she was breathing an hour ago.* It was determined there was nothing that would have prevented the patient from coding. However, there is that doubt or lack of confidence when you are inexperienced that causes second thoughts.

There was that brief thought, "these people let me be in charge!" In caring for the sick, these things are to be expected. At times, things seem to go bad for certain people. I believe it was the start of my black cloud. It would be a quiet week when the other night shift charge nurse was on, but when it was my week to work, any and everything that could go wrong usually did.

I got to know the ER physicians on the code team well. As time went on, when we had a code, he would call on the way up, see what was going on and say, "I knew you would be working, figures, last week was quiet."

# CHAPTER 7

## FIRE! DON'T RUN!

We all know that one coworker who never gets in a hurry or excited. One such coworker after being informed his patient was coding, slowly walks to the room while exclaiming, "well damn, I am not getting out of here on time this morning." I always said if we saw him running, do not ask questions, just get behind him and go. Well, one night this nurse comes running out of a patient's room screaming "**HIT THE BUTTON, HIT THE BUTTON**" over and over. This is usually interpreted as, hit the Code Blue Button. When I looked to see what room he came from, I realized this patient was a DNR. I tried to calm him down by informing him that she was a DNR. However, he kept running and screaming, with hands waving in the air, repeating, **"HIT THE BUTTON!"**. I could not get him to understand it was ok that she was a DNR, we did not have to code her. At this moment, another nurse runs by screaming, **"FIRE, FIRE!"** and pulls the fire alarm. This made me move much faster, realizing a room was on fire.

I called the operator to tell her to issue a Code Red, I assume she did not believe me since she said, "Are you sure? Are you kidding?" I answer, "Why yes, yes I am, I always wanted to call a Code Red in a hospital in the middle of the night. **NO I AM NOT KIDDING ROOM SO AND SO IS ON FIRE!!!!**

The aging heater in the room had caught fire, and flames were shooting about six feet high as we removed the patient from the room to safety. Was she thankful? No, she complained the whole time this room was not as big, she wanted her other room. Ungrateful, not at all thankful we kept her from burning to a crisp. We got the paper charts off the floor, per protocol, shut the doors, smoke was now starting to get thick and we placed wet towels under the door where the smoke was coming from.

The fire department shows up with NO equipment and in no particular hurry. In their defense, on a weekly basis a patient with dementia from the skilled unit would slip from their room and pull a fire alarm or call 911.

Sometimes the police would show up to investigate a report of assault or even murder. Therefore, the firemen had to hurry back to their truck, get their gear and then put out the fire. The room and its contents were a total loss. The patient was fine.

# CHAPTER 8

## Oh Say Can You See?

The hardest I have ever been hit was by an 80 something year old male patient who was in a wheelchair. He was suffering from dementia and threatening to sue me all night for everything under the sun. I bent down to unlock the break of his chair, when -- **SMACK, and I am seeing STARS**. He had slapped me across the cheek. Never under estimate the elderly little men and women they have the strength of Hercules and are as slick as Houdini. If one ever gets hold of a tender portion of skin or delicate body part expect to ask for assistance, because their hands become claws. That sweet little lady you loved on day shift, turns into the gremlin at night. Expect a few battle wounds.

# CHAPTER 9

## Being A Hostess/Babysitter

On this particular evening, my patient was a male well into his 80's. The daughter arrives late, near the end of visitation; with the wife who was also well into her 80s and suffering from late stage Alzheimer Disorder. After staying a few minutes, the daughter started giving me instructions on when to give medications while handing me a whole bag of medicines and physical therapy equipment. Confused I said, "Excuse me, we can't use these for your Dad". She said "No, they are for Mother" and proceeded to give me instructions when each was due and how to administer them since she was on her way home. I informed her that this was an ICU and that her father was the patient and I would not be responsible for the care of elderly mother.

The daughter looked me in the eyes and said, "Well what am I supposed to do with her, I wasn't prepared to keep mom tonight?" Well, I don't know but she can't stay here and that is your responsibility.

Well they left or so I thought. Later that evening I received a call from our PCU, asking had we lost a patient. The woman abandons her mother in our waiting room and goes home. The elderly woman was found wondering in and out of patients' rooms. It was later discovered that the mother suffered from Alzheimer's and needed supervision.

# CHAPTER 10

## Lost Then Found

Every nurse's fear is physically losing a patient. Patients will wander off for many reason's, including confusion, boredom, and just to cause trouble. It can be a source of extreme stress for hospital personnel when a patient goes missing.

On this particular night, regularly scheduled medication rounds result in a missing elderly man admitted that afternoon. I enter the room and the patient was gone. I notice immediately an open window and the worst comes to mind. I think, "OH MY GOD he's jumped." The unit is on the fourth floor. With trepidation, I make my way to the window and scan the ground below. Thank God, there was no body. I call security and we begin our search for the patient. In the end, we discovered he had taken the elevator to the ground floor, walked by security, through the ER and made his way to a small wooded area behind the hospital. He was unharmed, naked, very cold and clueless how he had gotten there.

# CHAPTER 11

## The Fear of God

Maybe you admit a patient to your floor, she is a post code from ICU. You step out just for a moment and go back in and she is in the bathroom, door locked, she won't answer you. Now I'm thinking, great, she just got here, she's locked herself in the bathroom and has coded. We had to call security and get them to unlock the door. We are ready to pounce with the crash cart, the door opens and she is sitting on the toilet, naked as the day she was born, only wearing black high top converse tennis shoes and her pulse ox probe tied to the hand railing, grinning and saying," you won't get me this time." Nothing will put the fear of God in you quicker than loosing a patient.

I'm going to just let you have a mental picture now about three nurses, a security officer and a naked elderly woman wrestling back to bed. Somehow, they get superhuman strength.

# CHAPTER 12

## May I Have Your Attention?

Now sometimes you have to wonder why people just do not use common sense. Sometimes you can get away with things on night shift that normally one could not on day shift.

The nursing assistant we had at night would constantly torture the hospital operator.
At least once a shift when he worked, sometime in the night you would hear, "May I have your attention please? May I have your attention please? Would Harry Butt please call the hospital operator? Would Harry Butt please call the hospital operator?"

I hope you are getting this name. I'm not going to comment further. Please, one would think after one or two shifts she would catch on. But, we were in West Virginia. I can say that, because I have a lot of family from West Virginia. (LOL)

# CHAPTER 13

## Wingardium Leviosa

Maybe you have patient's that think you are magic? My dear sweet mother was a patient at this hospital when she broke her leg and had to wear an external fixator. Which by the way, only the third time I saw my dad cry. The first time, was when my grandmother died and the second when I got married.

Now, my mom broke her leg. Which it only took me 30 years to realize, oh my God, they are not just my mom and dad. They are a man and woman who truly love each other and have the same feelings as young people do.

Now my mom is the kind of patient you love to have, mostly. Whatever the doctor says she is on it. She doesn't refuse anything. When the doctor says you need to be out of bed three times a day, she is calling the nurse at 0700 for her first time up and God help you if you are not in there.

Now using the bedpan was another story. My mom is a very private person. When she was informed she had to use a bedpan, she wouldn't let anyone else help her but me, but she wouldn't let me remove the covers or turn her over. In her words, "You are not going to see my naked behind". I am like mom, " I do not have my Harry Potter Wand so I cannot levitate you today." You are going to have to remove the covers and turn. I have seen hundreds of backsides.

I was promptly informed, "listen here little girl, you haven't seen mine and we aren't starting now".

# Chapter 14

## Gullible

Having a family member in this hospital brings with it a special kind of stress. However, when the emergency has passed or the surgery was successful it offers another way to relieve a little stress and get some payback on the little brother that pesters you constantly growing up. In my immediate family, I am the only member with a medical background. Most of most family will believe whatever I say when it comes to all things medical. After all, I am the *"nurse"*.

On this particular occasion, my brother was a patient. He had to have his lower leg amputated due to a hunting accident when he was in his 20's. His wife and myself, stayed with him the first night after surgery. He was confused from the drugs they had given him and sometime during the night, he insisted his foley be removed immediately. His wife was going to remove it, but he told her she did not know what she was doing, he was on my floor, therefore, I could take it out.

In his right mind, he would of been mortified by this. So thinking quickly and not missing an opportunity to prank my little brother, the idea came to mind.

The next day he was fine, surgery went well, he was up walking with crutches, non-weight bearing. He finally worked up the nerve to ask. He said, "Sis, I dreamed I asked you to take out my foley, please tell me you didn't?" Seeing how mortified he was, I thought briefly on telling him the truth then but I let it ride for a while. I said,"well, you asked, so I got permission and went ahead and took it out." He asked, "Did you see anything?" I said, "of course, you can't take it out blind folded." I let him think this most of the day, he could hardly look at me. Finally, his wife and I could not contain our laughter we caved.

Laughing, I said, "Bub, which was my name for him when we were little. Of course, I did not take it out. I would never do that." I just could not resist the temptation. I have never him more relieved. I just love my little brother. You know what they say though, "payback is a bitch".

# Chapter 15

## When There Is Nothing Left To Do But Laugh

In life, there are those moments when you have to detach, sit down and just watch. At the first hospital I worked, we had an orthopedic surgeon that was wonderful. His patients always faired really well mainly because he is very particular about post-operative care and patient cooperation.

On this particular day, the doctor goes into the patient's room to find him very confused and thinking the doctor is there to attack him. He comes hobbling out of his room, with an external fixator on one leg and swinging his crutches in a circle above his head while yelling **HELP! HELP!**

The five-foot tall doctor is running behind him also yelling, "Sir, You must come back! You must come back!" Behind them both is a nurse shouting at the doctor, "Watch the crutches!" It's a real life scene from a Tom and Jerry Cartoon.

They complete two laps around the entire unit when the patient runs back in his room sits down and acts as if nothing has happened. The patient remembered nothing and swore we made the whole thing up. Sometimes there is nothing left to do but laugh.

# Chapter 16

## Finders, Keepers....

Have you ever forgotten where you parked your car? I walked out with a friend one morning and she could not find her truck. I laughed and accused her of getting old. I really felt bad when she discovered her truck had been stolen, a car ring had come through and stole several vehicles out of the hospital parking lot, Including one brand new BMW convertible owned by the ER physician.

A few days later, they found her truck gutted. Luckily, her insurance paid and all was well. I do not think the BMW was found. See? Drive clunkers to work. You will never have to worry about a stolen car.

# Chapter 17

## Cute Little Grannies

Here is some free advice for new nurses. At first, you won't want to restrain patients, but you will get over it real quick. Moreover, looks can be deceiving with cute little grannies.

I had a sweet little woman who was very confused and we had placed a Posey Vest for her safety. A posey vest is like a sleeveless jacket that ties at the waist that can be secured to a bed or chair. When I re-enter the room later granny has somehow obtained a pair of scissors and has not only cut off her vest, but has cut it into perfect square quilting pieces. The pieces were arranged into neat little piles. Her sewing basket left by concerned family. They had wanted to give her something to occupy her time during her stay.

Luckily, granny was not aggressive and really was very sweet and handed over her scissors stating, "ok I'm done for now." I put the scissors back in her sewing basket and quietly returned it to her family.

FYI, Please remind families not to give sharp objects to a confused, elderly patient. Remember, as a nurse you are responsible for what happens to that patient in all cases.

Those cute little grannies are the same ones that when the sun goes down there heads spin and possessed by demons. They can't be trusted. They pinch, kick, hit, bite when you least expect it. Be especially careful of those fingernails that turn into claws after midnight. You may be yelling for someone to come and try to break that super human grip from your top or pants. I have had several scrub tops ripped and pants too by one of those cute little grannies.

 Of course, this is the side of the dear sweet patient, that family members never see. Families are often surprised that grandma or grandpa can out curse a sailor. Or, the cute little grandpa who is in four point restraints, but manages to remove them and his central line and his Intraventricular Drain (EVD) in seconds.

I saw his hand go up at the door and I'm running, yelling **NO DON'T PULL ON THAT**. And it's out. I said, "Honey look what you've done?" The patient replies, "I know, I know, I knew I wasn't supposed to do that when you started yelling at me". He also informs me, "well at least you were Johnny on the spot", and I said, "no, no I wasn't. If I was, you would still have your drain in."

Then I said, "Now I have call the neurosurgeon and he isn't going to be happy." Not missing a beat, my confused little patient said "Well, everyone needs a little excitement in their lives." Actually, no, no I don't. And of course the first question asked is "Why wasn't he restrained?" Really?

Needless to say, he wasn't happy.  Upon further evaluation he didn't really pull it out, he broke the drain leaving about five inches still in his brain.   Neurosurgery was even happier when I told him the trauma doctor removed the rest of the drain.  **And**, even  happier still, when I told him he threw it away, so I don't know if the tip was intact.  Well, all was well, they spoke, they found the drain with the tip intact.   Just saying, I made that doctors night. (LOL)

# Chapter 18

## With Dignity

Now as a nurse you see people at their best, at their worst, you see life and death, both good and bad for each. You see people recover and leave the hospital and return to a normal life and those that live (technically) that never move anything but their eyes where the week before they were active athletes, mothers, fathers. They were playing for their school or with their children.

Now all they can do is curl up in a protracted fetal position and live or exist in a drooling and posturing body that wastes away often lying for days in their own wastes because the family is unable or unwilling to provide care and have to rely on the minimal care of long care facilities.

See these poor souls are frequent flyers and are seen on a regular basis when they fall and endure open fractures for whole days or lie in body fluids in the same position and suffer from pressure induced softball sized open infected ulcers often eating flesh to the bone. You see a broad spectrum of patients both the best and worst that humanity can produce.

So how do you get up and continue to work 12 and 16 hour shifts in this environment? You have to have a sense of humor in all this sadness.

# Chapter 19

## Walking Dead

If one works in the healthcare field, especially a hospital, it is not good to be afraid of a dead body. Most certainly, one should never allow co-workers to gain this knowledge. One of my first and dearest friends and fellow nurse was one such person. We responded to a patient's room when we discovered the cardiac monitor showed asystole or no heartbeat. The woman had made the decision when she was lucid to forgo any resuscitative measures when the time came for her to die. In the industry, this is referred to as a "Do Not Resuscitate (DNR)" order. One of the first thing's any healthcare worker learns is to treat the patient and not the monitor. The patient was unresponsive, not breathing with no pulse and declared deceased by a physician. At this point, nursing usually takes over and prepares the body by removing any medical apparatus and making the body presentable to the family. My friend and I offer our help and set about the task. We were almost finished when the deceased woman, slowly begins to rise off the bed about foot as if to sit up, expels a long breath of air in a low heart stopping moan then abruptly falls back to the bed.

Before I can react at all, I hear an almost inaudible chirp and hear footsteps of someone running down the hall. I quickly follow in her foot- steps. In between uncontrolled bursts of laughter, the experienced nurse explains this is called the, "Lazarus Effect." Sometimes a dead body will spontaneously expel the last bit of gases trapped in the lungs and because it usually happens just as rigor mortis is setting in the body will contract slightly at the waist making the torso rise. Even armed with this knowledge when it happens it is still spooky. After the incident my friend confesses to us, her aversion to dead bodies, and this particular occurrence made matters worse.

We did at every opportunity use this knowledge to help our friend face her fears. Our hospital endeavored to show respect and give privacy as much as possible even requiring the transport bed to transfer the deceased to the morgue. This did qualify as a means to prank our friend without involving any ones loved one.

The hospital's policy required a nurse to retrieve a stretcher from the morgue. Another nurse and I volunteered. When we get back to the floor, I climb into the stretcher, closed the covering and the other nurse pushes me into the room. Our friend had just finished with her preparations and was waiting for her opportunity to leave the room.

As she walks by the stretcher to leave the room, I reach out and lightly grab a hand. At this point all hell breaks loose as she releases a blood-curdling scream and I am all most positive her feet do not touch the floor until she reaches the far wall of the hall.  I thought for sure she was going to pass out after she hit the wall.

# Chapter 20

## Let It Go

The following is the perfect example why physicians should notify the family their loved one has expired. Near the end of my tenure at my first hospital I took part in a code-blue where we worked hard to save this lady, but after 45 minutes, the physician ended (called) the code, and gave the time of death.

It is customary to administer certain drugs during resuscitative efforts such as epinephrine and atropine that have prolonged stimulating effects on the body well after such efforts cease. The doctor phones the patient's son, explains the evening's events and informs him in spite of every effort his mother passed away.

In the meantime, we are removing IV's, heart monitor, the only thing left was just the breathing tube when I think I see her cheek move. My coworkers think I am crazy until they also see her move. Closer examination reveals shallow breathing and a normal sinus rhythm.

When the doctor is informed, he looks at me very seriously and says, "What am I supposed to do? I've already told her family she is dead." Well, I do not know sir, but you better come down here.

So he comes into the room and is telling us to bag her, we gently remind him the cart has already been taken away and we have nothing on the floor. I look around and he has his hands cupped around the ET tube and is blowing into it. You do what you have to do. We get her stabilized enough for a transport to ICU and he calls the son back to tell him, his mother is **not** dead.

None of us stuck around for that next conversation. Unfortunately, shortly after arriving in the ICU the woman coded again. The epinephrine and other drugs given during the code provided enough stimuli to the woman's body for it to function until they were exhausted. Soon the doctor was informing the family for the second time that evening their mother was dead. That is why they make the big bucks.

# Chapter 21

## New Beginning

After three and half years, I left my comfort zone to seek employment elsewhere. Economic conditions in the rural region I worked took a turn for the worse. This mandated a family move to an area with better work opportunities for my husband. There was a nationwide shortage of nurses and hospitals were aggressively recruiting, and offering large sign-on bonuses. I had no trouble in securing interviews.

Every advertisement I applied too, I was immediately offered a position with my choice of shift. At this point in my nursing career, I had become a hopeless adrenaline and trauma junky. Therefore, I accepted a position in the Neuro/Trauma Intensive Care Unit of a Large Level I Trauma Center. (Watching every episode of ER had nothing to do with this.) LOL.

I now have three and a half years of experience. I am beginning to feel comfortable in my nursing skills. In addition, I am use to taking care of ventilators and been through several code blues. Keep in mind at my old hospital when patients became "really sick," they were shipped off to the ICU.

For those readers not aware the NTICU has been establish to take the most serious patients with neurological or trauma related injuries. Some examples would be head injuries, stabbings, gunshot wounds, assaults, spinal cord injuries, amputated limbs, and so on. NTICU nurses are only allowed a maximum of two patients. In many instances the nurse may only have one patient to care for during an entire shift. The low ratio is primarily due to the severe and unstable conditions of most NTICU patients. In rare cases, I have actually seen a patient require as many as six nurses, several physicians and other specialist health personnel to keep them alive.

There is not enough paper to write down all the interesting nights and patients I have seen in 15 years of working Neuro/Trauma. I would like to share those that have really stood out in my mind over the years.

Now I am a new nurse with three and half years' experience starting in a Neuro/Trauma ICU and it is my first day. A few hours into the shift, I realize something; I DON'T KNOW SHIT. My God, what was I thinking working in an ICU? These people are really, really, sick. I never considered there could be patients so sick they were a 1:1 or at times a 6:1 nurse to patient ratio. I don't like change and I am definitely out of my comfort zone. Reality set in when my first patient coded, and I thought, "uh-oh, I am the ICU they are not going anywhere."

# Chapter 22

## Russian Roulette??

My first night off orientation, I am feeling a little more confident with some training, I think, "this isn't so bad. I can do this."  Hoping I have left the "Black Cloud" behind me, I start my shift thinking, "WOW, I work in a Neuro/Trauma ICU.  I have only one patient it's going to be great.

Then I hear **GOLD ALERT-ETA 12 Minutes** over the PA speakers. A Gold Alert is code telling anyone that is involved that a known severe injury is in route to the hospital and has an estimated time of arrival (ETA) of 12 minutes.  Since I am the lucky nurse with only one patient, I will get the patient if they are admitted to the NTICU. The first report I receive is it's a self-inflicted gunshot wound to the head.  As a little more filters up, I learn the patient is a 19 year old, who apparently lost while playing Russian Roulette.

I receive word that I will be admitting the patient and immediately go into mild panic mode. However, I tell myself, "I am OK, I can handle this Gold, I can do this.  I have had six weeks of orientation and I am an experienced nurse.  I get report from the ER nurse, she informs me the kid is brain dead and the family has refused to accept this.

When the neuro-surgeon spoke with the mom, she threw a glass of water in his face, accusing him of "not fixing my son because he is black...". This surgeon is direct and to the point and very understanding when speaking to families. Wiping the water from his face, he said, *"No ma'am, it's not because he is black, it's because I am not God."*

The doctor calls me and says, "This kid is dead, there is nothing else to do. When he gets to the unit finish infusing the three bags of normal saline. When that wears off he will code and when he does you tell those medicine residents to do one and I repeat "ONE" round of CPR (cardiopulmonary resuscitation) and then call it". (Actual quote)

As I am getting him situated, I turn to see four of the largest men I have ever seen, their arms crossed looking down at me. The largest of the four says in an intimidating voice, "You are going to fix him right?" I politely excuse myself and walk out the door, and then RUN. My co-workers call security and promptly have them removed.

Just as the neurosurgeon had predicted, when the fluid boluses wore off, he codes, and dies. The trauma resident goes and speaks with the family to let them know. They come back and say their good byes. Lots of family. After cleaning the patient and while I am calling the Medical Examiner, I notice a young girl and older woman entering the unit, and start to go into the deceased patient's room. I am too late, to catch the young girl, she has already entered the room, after a second or two, she proceeds to slam doors and scream at the very top of lungs.  I catch the woman and find that she is the mother, she has just arrived and had no idea what happened other than her son had been shot.  Of course, there is no doctor present, and the young girl is now rolling on the floor screaming.  I have to inform the mother," I'm sorry ma'am, your son died about an hour ago."  She drops like a stone and hits the floor, fainted.  All the family came back, but no one told us his mother had left to get clothes to stay with her son.

We call security on the young girl, when she becomes combative and so unwilling to communicate.  We find she is 14 years of age and pregnant with the patients second child.   This is the first time I informed a family member their loved one passed.  It leaves a heavy feeling and one the hardest things I ever had to do.  A parent,  no matter the circumstances, should have to lose a child, especially a loving mother.  The cry of a mother will haunt you forever.  It is a different, mournful cry and unlike any other.

That was my first night off orientation.  Welcome to the Neuro/Trauma ICU, I guess my black cloud did come with me after all and was waiting for the right time to reveal itself.

# Chapter 23

## Still Learning

Now when I first started here, our visiting hours were 8:30 to 2:00 pm and then again from 4:30 to 8:30 pm, Two people at a time and no one under 13 years allowed. No one spent the night unless it was a pediatric patient or the patient was actively dying. Some people think a broken arm is actively dying. I was taught on orientation, when visiting hours were over, you went in and reminded the family and asked them to leave.

Being new and coming from a floor, I was mortified to have to do this. Trust me, that is something you quickly get over. I did, very quickly. I learned very fast that working in a trauma unit, you have drama. So much drama that its not even funny. I guess it comes with the clientele. Now our visiting hours are 9 am to 8:30 pm, still two at a time, no one under 13. Only one parent stays if a pediatric patient. No one spends the night unless actively dying. (Unless they are insistent then one person may stay).

Over the years, it still amazes me that no matter how sick these people are, on ventilator's, multiple IV medications, some even with EVD's (intraventricular drains) for monitoring pressure in the brain. No matter how many time's you ask them not to touch, or to be quiet, brain injuries need no stimulation. What is the first thing they do? Visitor's look and say "ok", then proceed to shake the patient, kiss them on the mouth (even with tubes and sputum and other things running out).

When you have the flu at home, you feel bad, you want to be left alone. So "COME ON PEOPLE", if you feel bad with the flu, imagine how your loved one feels with everything broken and drains coming out of every orifice.

LEAVE THEM ALONE, trust us, we will let you know when it's ok to harass them. That would be when they are starting to harass us. LOL.

Seriously, brain injuries are a whole different ball game. The brain needs quiet time to heal. If they are having high pressures in their brain, they really don't need stimulation.

# CHAPTER 24

## When Pigs Fly

Now we all have superstitions we hear some people really believe in. This other patient we had, who was a fall, bad head injury. Now his family, who was very simple, not meant in a bad way. They had no medical knowledge, very country. I walk into the room, and I'm like, "Are those real animal teeth?" They were very forthcoming and very proud that "yes, they were hog's teeth." They swore they woke up and saw a hog flying by the window and thought this meant good luck. So they slaughtered the hog, and brought the teeth in and hung them up for good luck. Not kidding.

# Chapter 25

## Thrown Under The Bus

One of my first friends I made when I started this unit was a blast to work with. Even though she later left and moved to Florida, I still keep in touch with her. I think I'm the discussion of a few tales there.

I'm not sure what most nurse's work across the country but our hospital is mainly 12 hour shifts. Now I work one 16 hour shift and two 12 hour shifts, because I live an hour away and I only want to drive three days a week. This is great, except the two years we had to do mandatory overtime.

Anyway, I come in at three pm and I am getting report from my friend. Just as she finishes up with report, I realize my patient is coming back from her procedure being pushed, quickly down the hall, they are practically running with the bed and she is accompanied by several nurses and three physicians.

I look at her and ask, "Why are they running?" and she politely and quickly informs me, "I don't know, but it can't be good. See ya" tomorrow and leaves. Needless to say they bust through the door and she's coding and I bring the crash cart along. She was young, early 20's. We really did try for a very long time to save up, but she had so many issues against her and in the end it was called.

I found out after the fact that my friend indeed did not leave me. She was out comforting the family and letting them know we were doing everything possible and keeping them up to date. She even stayed and helped do post mortem care.

Also, in our unit, because it is a closed unit, admissions have to have a critical care consult. Either surgical critical care or pulmonary critical care. This one admission, I threw our resident under the bus. When I was explaining they needed to have a critical care consults, I informed him, "We can do surgery critical care, he is standing right here, would you like to speak with him?" Sorry, we like dealing with our own residents. We know they will take excellent care of our patients. So I did, I threw him right under that bus.

We are reminded, every day we come to work how precious life is.

When it count's we are there for you and we work great as a team. I'm sure most places are this way. I wish you could see our trauma unit. When it comes down to the count, we are so good as a team, everyone just jumps in and does the job.

We don't have to say," you do this or that." We have been together so long, we just know and we do it. I think we are a pretty, awesome team. I know our unit has laughed with the families and cried with the families. When it counts we are there.

# CHAPTER 26

## Out of Control

We now have locked doors in our unit thanks to me. Because a family member went all "BAD", she attacked me from the back and hit me twice in the head. Looking back, I suppose this is funny now. With visitors yelling, "I'll be your witness and the flight crew saying, you can take her". Violence in the hospital is increasing and is not funny. I always joke and say "I took one for the team", as we now have locked doors. My friend always advises me, "Keep your back to the door and feet on the floor." Not long after this incident, I had another one. Like I said, "Black Cloud" in every sense of the word.

I'm taking care of this woman, and her son is visiting. He is pacing around the room, wide eyed. Kind of like a caged animal talking about how he needs Ativan, etc.

He grabbed my arm and demanded I get him Ativan. I politely informed him I could not and if he was sick he needed to go to the ER. I left the room to call security.

He also left the room, we thought he was gone until the nurse from our PCU called.

He had barricaded hisself into our conference room, was smoking and demanding Ativan. Not sure how long it took for security to get him out. Again, things they don't teach in nursing school. Always be alert and be careful.

# Chapter 27

## Well Known By the ME

In a Level I trauma unit most deaths require the involvement of a medical examiner (ME). Part of the ME's work up requires the taking of pictures One of our beloved ME's, who always comes in when we have death, I was holding the patient over for him to take pictures, etc. I was like, Dr. M, I was just wondering how many pictures you have with my boobs and stomach in them? He laughed and said he kept them for several years, but that's not the problem, just think how many has been shown in court.

I also told him I did not know how I felt about him calling the unit and recognizing my voice. I answer Hello, Neuro/Trauma ICU May I help you? He will always say Hi, then ask, "you have this patient?" He told me, "look at it this way, at least if you are ever found in a ditch, you'll be easily identified." That does not makes me feel any better.

# CHAPTER 28

## Proof

How many health care workers believe visitors should show ID, Marriage license, etc.? I firmly believe that. One of the things I hate most is a liar.

As this story begins you will come to see why, because I surely thought we are all going to jail. My patient who was very sick, or one of them, I should say.

The family decided to withdraw support. His son, some brothers and sisters and extended family were present in the room. I asked, was he married? The son said," he was but he has been divorced for several years now". I'm still asking, legally divorced, because if not, she is still his decision maker.

ALL family assured me he was. We withdraw support, the patient dies, while I'm waiting for the resident to come and pronounce, I received a phone call. Who do you think it is??? I'm asked, "Does this hospital make a habit out of withdrawing support on a patient without the spouses permission??"

I'm not quite sure what I said to her. I hang up and immediately call legal (not caring it's the middle of the night) to let them know what happened.

Then I went into the room and started , not yelling, BUT VERY STRONGLY VOCALIZING, what the hell?? You lied, he is married. You can't do that, it is illegal. They could go to jail, etc., etc. Then he starts yelling," that Bitch isn't getting a thing I'll burn the house down first." Remember I said drama with trauma.

On another occasion, I have an intubated patient getting ready to go for emergency surgery. His wife signs consents, she leaves. A while later I get a call from our PCU, a nurse out there (later she comes to work in our unit) informs me several people are here to see so and so. She asks if his wife can visit? I'm like his wife has already been here, she's left I don't know who these people are.

Well this lady starts crying and the nurse comes back demanding to know why his wife can't visit. I explain that's not his wife, his wife had already been here.

 Well, well, well, low and behold guess what?? Yep you guessed it. This woman IS his wife, his legal wife, the other was his girlfriend, which she didn't know anything about until now, thanks to me.  So that's a mess. And not to mention, but all six visitors had trach scars and were very proud they had all survived accidents at one time or another. Just saying. Tree, straight, no branches. So I am a firm believer, all ICU's should have lie detectors, documents, etc.

# Chapter 29

## The Jokester

No matter where you work there seems to be that one co-worker with whom everyone enjoys working. The one that seemingly makes the shift go by much faster and can be counted on to bring a smile to your face no matter how bad the shift.

It started out with her decorating Fred.   Fred is a two foot tall skeleton that sits on the unit nurses' desk.  Every holiday, Fred would get an outfit to match the occasion. St. Patrick's Day was the best, because Fred got a Fedora (empty versed vial),a Beer (a decorated soda can), and an insulin syringe in between his radius and ulna bones.  Fred was a drunk and a druggie.

I cannot begin to tell how many times this girl, we will call her Mindy, pulled pranks on us.  Once when retrieving a blanket from the warmer she jumps out just as I open the door and scares me silly.  On another occasion, I admitted a brain dead patient that had committed a terrible crime and thus had a bad reputation.  Knowing of my religious background and belief in after life she turns the side light in my patient's room on and points it toward a red trash can making the room have a red eerie glow.  She then proceeds to inform me that the devil has come for my patient. It freaked me out a little I have to say.

I also had a patient that had been on pressors for days. They had caused his *fingers to mummify. They were black, very hard. I was afraid if I hit one, it would* break off.

Well, Mindy went and got casting supplies made a fake finger, painted it black, put it in the bed with the patient. I asked her to help me turn him, and when I went to pull him, she screamed and pointed to the bed. I saw it laying there and thought it had fell off. She's laughing and I'm yelling oh my god, oh my god, I broke his finger.

Mindy would also go to the break room, pick a nurse, call her and act like a family member demanding to know information, but saying she had no pass word. There are so many pranks she has pulled over the years, this is another benefit of working night shift.

You know how they say Karma has everyone's address? Well the time finally came for someone to get her back. One of our nurses was pregnant in the unit and expecting any time. Mindy was terrified, she was going to go into labor at work. Our pregnant nurse rigged a juice box and a piece of tubing inside of her pant leg and asked Mindy for help turning a patient.

Mindy wouldn't let her pull so she pulled the patient and as the other nurse bent over, she squeezed the juice box allowing red liquid to flow down her leg onto the floor.

Mindy assumes her water has busted and immediately begins to call for help. We ignore the plea for help and she finds us all laughing as she comes to scold us for not helping. Finally, someone got her back. Mindy is in every sense a great nurse and was good to have in an emergency situation. She takes great care of her patients and has since moved on to administrative position in another hospital. We miss her very much.

Mindy never spared the residents or doctors either. Once, when we still used paper charting she filled out a complete fake and false record showing abnormal blood pressures in the 40's, temperatures of 104 and 105 and no urinary output. When the resident rounded in the morning and saw this all she could say was "Why didn't anyone call me"?

She was so fun to work with and made the night go by fast. There was never a dull moment when working with Mindy.

# CHAPTER 30

## Hank

Within the unit I work, **we** assist with a large number of organ donations.  Donations can be a very trying and difficult decision for a grieving family to make. It is a wonderful gift and I personally encourage everyone to donate.  This little story is in no way what so ever meant to minimize the unselfish act of those that make the decision to donate.  It also does not judge or belittle those who do not choose to do so.

With all donation scenarios representatives from an organ procurement team speak with the family.  Families are encouraged to ask questions, clearly understand what donation is and what is involved.  Sometimes this is not enough and hence my story of Hank.

On this occasion, the procurement team spoke with a particularly large family about a beloved male family member.  The family was informed that their loved one was "brain dead" and that he may be eligible for donation. The family seemed to be unusually saddened and concerned with the news. Actually, not everyone that wishes to can qualify for donation. Potential donors are rigoursly screened and must undergo a battery of tests and meet very specific criteria before being approved. With approval, there may still only be one or two body parts that qualify and approved. This and more was covered with the family. The family had few questions and only requested some time to discuss this among themselves. The team was called back after a short time. They were very quiet and most eyes wet from tears except for the two oldest brothers. The next to oldest brother had evidently been chosen speaker for the rest, and he had only one word to say, "Hank."

The team looked at each other puzzled and back to the speaker and to the oldest brother who had stepped closer to the bed. "We do not understand sir, will Hank be making the decision?" asked a team member. The man looked at his sick family member for long second and then at Hank and back to us with all the seriousness in the world and said, "we have decided that it will be Hank that will donate his brain." I simply turned and walked out of the room feeling very guilty and sorry for the procurement team I left behind.

# CHAPTER 31

## The Attack

We were all sitting around the nursing desk charting one night when all of a sudden we hear a scream. We jump up, run into the room, and ask the nurse what is wrong? What is wrong? She replies, "There was a stink bug on the pillow, it was just staring like it was going to attack me, Really!" We have never let her live this down, the attack of the killer stink bug.

# CHAPTER 32

## Always Have a Plan

Always have a plan. I am a firm believer in always be prepared. I learned this early on as a Charge Nurse. I perform a little ritual like getting charting done, medicines given, etc. . All those things that can be done need to get done early, because you never know when something is going to happen.

On one particular night, we had several bad patients. Therefore, I did my usual routine. I informed the staff what was going on and if this person coded, you three go help her and if my patient codes the remaining three come help me. I had everything prepared I thought.

Well it happened, both coded within a few seconds of each other and the resident standing in the middle of the station telling us what to do and us telling him they are in this rhythm, no this rhythm. Unbelievably it all went very smoothly. Again, always have a plan. Things change at the drop of a hat.

## Chapter 33

## ER in The House

Who has watched the television show ER?  Well I did faithfully every Thursday night.   It was just coming on when I started nursing school.

My patient was doing very badly and I had spoken with the family about DNR status and so forth.  They were asking, what I thought were appropriate questions.  The patient was being given the maximum amount of blood pressure medicine possible, his skin was mottled, and his blood pressure was still in the 60's.  As serious as can be, they asked could we not do what they do on ER to save him?  Well, not missing a beat, I politely informed them we have done everything ER does and a little more.  Then I stepped out.  This unfortunate gentleman did not make it and his family got into a fight over who was going to get his earring.  Kid you not.

# Chapter 34

## Stalker

Surely, everyone has had a stalker in their career. I've had two. One, kind of scary and the other funny. My first one was from the lab. It started when she drew blood from an arterial line that took the residents several hours to place. She drew blood and didn't flush and it clotted off.

Lab made me write it up. After that, she would follow me around into patients rooms and would tell me "I'm watching you" or "I know what you drive".
This ended up with my manager and her manager and us having a meeting. Things were said, statements taken, and I'm not sure what happened, but I never saw her again.

The second, was a resident who would follow me around everywhere. I do mean everywhere. We were still using paper charts at this time, and he would take them and leave the floor and we were forever looking for them. So, in the mornings, in order to finish my work, I would take the charts and go hide in the bathroom to finish up. It would not be long until I could hear him asking for me, which by the way he pronounced my name wrong. Next thing I know, I hear a knock on the bathroom door and someone saying, "Charge-Nurse, are you in there? Can I come in? Ms. Nurse can you hear me?"

This is the same physician I called when his patient was ready to code and informing him that his patient was mottled and blue, at which he laughs saying, "Mottled?, what is this word? I must learn this word mottled, funny".

We also had a stat CT scan one morning on a patient and as I leave the floor, and pushing the bed down the hall he stops us and takes the chart He decides he wants to review it before we go. My co-worker looks at him and says, "You have five seconds to relinquish that chart or loose your hand". He just could not understand the situation was emergent, the patient blew a pupil and that neurosurgery was waiting. I needed to go and he just didn't get it.

# Chapter 35

## Fight!! Fight!!

Sometimes you just get to be the referee. It was the middle of January, very cold, snow on the ground. We had a patient die. His family, very nice came to say their good byes.

It wasn't long, and I received a call from the PCU, our sister unit, saying, "One of your family members if fighting in the waiting room". Well, we call security and it was the nice family. Two of the patient' sons were fist fighting in our waiting room.

After security separated them, all the fuss was over who was going to dig the grave. I kid you not. Due to the weather, they were fighting over who was going to have to dig the grave.

# Chapter 36

## Ride'Em Cowboy

On this particular night, the unit was very busy. Many of our patients were unstable, just a lot going on.

One patient in particular was having many issues and was on a roto-rest bed. This bed, as you know, automatically turns while keeping the spine straight.

Well this patient coded, as usual, we all rush in, stop the bed, doing what we do during a code and the physician walks in and wants to know why is the bed off. Really?? The nurse who has the patient informs him we are doing chest compressions. The physician informs us we do not have to stop the bed. So, we restarted the bed, it's automatically turning and visualize if you will. Here we are, the nurse is doing chest compressions on this bed, with the bed turning, the whole time the code is in progress.

You go M, he managed to stay on the bed the whole time, Ride'Em Cowboy.

Now just imagine, you are walking by this room, and you glance in and all you see is M going up and down, slowly, while doing chest compressions. I'm not quite sure how he managed to stay on. You go M.

# Thank You

Let me just say I truly enjoy being a nurse. Working with residents and all of the healthcare team. They have taught me so much over the years and I hope I have perhaps, taught them something too.

I have seen many residents come and go through the years. They feel like my children, watching them come in that first year, hesitant, some shy, some cocky (LOL), and watching them grow and learn over the years.

Then they leave strong, independent, intelligent physicians. So many I could name over the years, some I remain in touch with, others go and we never hear from again, but always wishing them the best of luck.

Thank you to all the residents I have worked with over the years. Each has been a blessing in their own way and maybe ever so often, a pain in my butt, but, we could not be a team without all of you. Thank you for what you do. Thank you to all my co-workers, respiratory, PT/OT, speech, physicians, dietary, housekeeping, etc. EVERYONE who plays a role in the patient's welfare, if it were not for all of us, this would not work. We are a TEAM.

## Just Some Thoughts...

Remember, I'm a nurse not a writer. I hope everyone who has read this book has enjoyed these stories. They are just a few memories I have over the years.

I continue to work in the Neuro/Trauma Intensive Care Unit at my hospital. It's been over 15 years and I love it here. I love my co-workers and truly could not imagine working any place else. I love the adrenaline, the trauma, the patients, and most times even their families.

Please remember, to always have respect and dignity for your patients. Treat them, as you would want to be treated with the utmost compassion. Cry with your patients, and their families because it is one of those things which makes you human. We nurses are their advocates in what is most often the worse times of their lives. We are sometimes the only voice they have. Be protective of your patient, question what and who you do not understand.

When you become indifferent and cannot cry, be empathetic, feel, or question, perhaps then it's time to remove your-self from patient care. Always be open to change, and new ideas.

Again, I hope you enjoyed these stories. They were in no way, intended to make fun of anyone. They are just memories from my nursing career that stood out over the years.

A big thank you to those physicians and residents, who I work with on a daily basis, I appreciate what you do. I enjoy learning and working side by side with you. After all, we are trying to achieve the same goal for our patients.

Remember The Three A's of Success:

**AVAILABILITY, AFFABILITY AND ABILITY**
-If you're not available to help patients and colleagues, If you're not easy to get along with, Then it doesn't matter how much ability you have, you won't succeed. –Dr. Christopher C. Baker, MD, Six Blue ducks, 2014

*In Summary,*

Nurses have and lead very demanding lives. We work with doctors, treating patients, and educate communities, are just a few of the responsibilities nurses perform on a daily basis.

In fact, you could say that nurses are the backbone of our health care system.

Sometimes nursing can be challenging. We spend holidays at work and not with our families. Missing milestones in our children's lives because we are making sure your mom, dad, brother, sister, or child is getting their medicines and the things they need to help them recover.

It can be exhausting mentally and physically, but the knowledge and power to help treat others is what keeps us going in challenging times. And just everyone now and then, that patient that comes back, that you thought would never recover, comes back to see you and thank you for all you did. He/she remembers that kind word, or the encouragement you gave the family. That is why we do it.

And while nurses are strong spirited, positive and focused even nurses need a little pick me up every once in a while.

So, please enjoy these little humerous stories.

*A Few Quotes…*

*The character of a nurse is just as important as the knowledge he/she possesses. (Carolyn Jarvis, Inspiration Quotes for Nurses)*

*Our job as nurses is to cushion the sorrow and celebrate the job, every day, while we are "just doing our jobs." (Christine Belle, Inspirational Quotes for Nurses.)*

*People will forget what you said, they will forget what you did, but they will never forget how you made them feel.* (Maya Angelou Inspiration Nursing Quotes)

Bio


Lesia Yates, went to at a small community college, then to a larger university. I have two degrees. I'm currently working toward my Bachelor's degree and studying to take my CCRN and CNRN. I continue to work in the Neuro/Trauma ICU as charge nurse and occasionally orient new staff. I have 18 years' experience as a Registered Nurse.
I currently live with my husband of 29 years and her two Sons, who are currently pursuing degrees in the medical field.

Printed in Great Britain
by Amazon.co.uk, Ltd.,
Marston Gate.